Quilling for Beginners

10 PROJECTS TO SHAPE AND MAKE YOUR OWN

LEISURE ARTS, INC. • Maumelle, Arkansas

INTRODUCTION

A forgotten artform, that originated in England and quickly spread to the American Colonies, is making its way back into the hearts of artists everywhere. That artform you ask? Quilling.

Quilling is a specific technique where an artist chooses paper strips and has an end goal of creating various designs by adhering paper to a background. Each paper strip rolled, shaped, and glued will help bring your vision to life.

In this book, you will find a step-by-step guide of everything you need to help get you started on your quilling project, as well as a collection of 10 quilling designs to make your own. You will also find full-size patterns to help you create your own artwork.

Regardless of age or skill level, you can make your way through all the projects in this book. They will be an amazing addition to your home and a unique gift for everyone you love.

TABLE OF CONTENTS

Daisy Bouquet....................................page 3
The Cats are in Love............................page 6
Ice Cream Cactus................................page 9
Floral Heart...page 12
Modern Roses......................................page 15
Dolphin and Waves.............................page 17
Whale Tail..page 20
Floral Elephant....................................page 23
The Quilled Mandala..........................page 26
Coffee...page 30
Patterns..page 34
General Instructions...........................page 40
Meet Alyona Kochubey.....................page 47

Daisy Bouquet

SHOPPING LIST

- ☐ Paper strips 5-10 mm (¼" to ⅜") wide: yellow, white, and green
- ☐ 5" x 7" piece of watercolor paper for background
- ☐ Scissors
- ☐ Tweezers
- ☐ Ruler for measuring
- ☐ Tape for tracing
- ☐ Elmer's® Glue-All® Multi-Purpose Glue Extra Strong Formula
- ☐ ¼" - ⅜" wide ribbon for bow
- ☐ Metal embossing stylus (optional)
- ☐ Pencil (optional)
- ☐ 5" x 7" piece of black cardstock for background (optional)
- ☐ Frame with 5" x 7" opening (optional)

Instructions

***Note:** Follow **Curling**, page 43, to curl each strip before shaping.*

1. If black background is desired, glue the black cardstock to the watercolor paper.
2. Follow **Tracing**, page 42, to transfer pattern, page 37, to the background.
3. For a flower center, follow **Loose Coil**, page 44, and use a 5½" yellow paper strip to make a Loose Coil. Make a total of 5 Loose Coils. Squeeze each flower center in the middle to make an oval **(Fig. 1)**.

Fig. 1

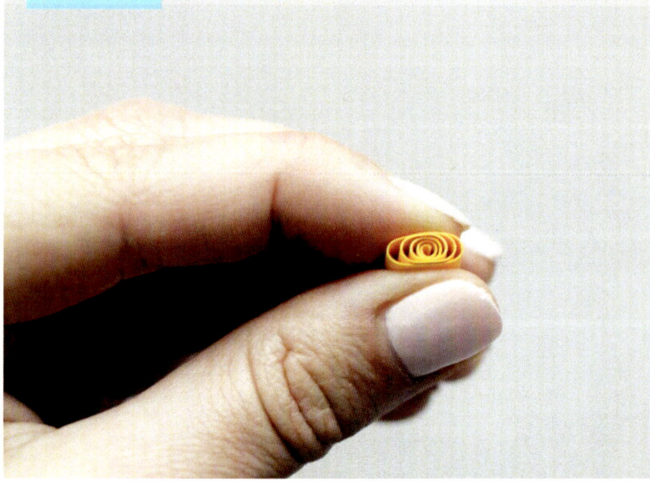

4. Glue the flower centers to the background in the center of the petals (**Fig. 2**).

Fig. 2

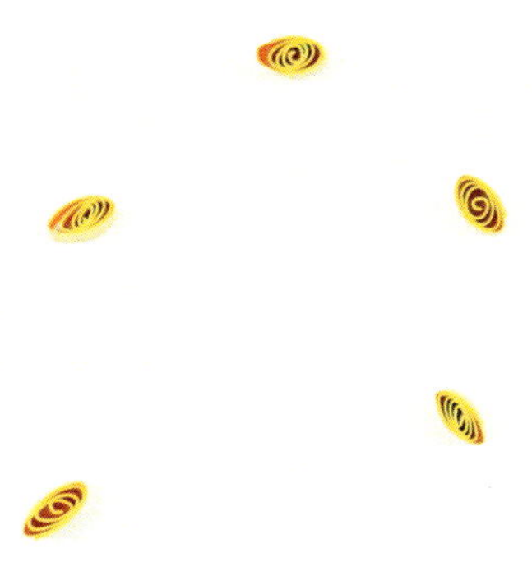

5. For petals, cut 1" white paper strips. You'll need about 13 - 15 petals for the whole flowers and about 8 petals for the partial flower. Curl the paper piece (**Fig. 3**).

Fig. 3

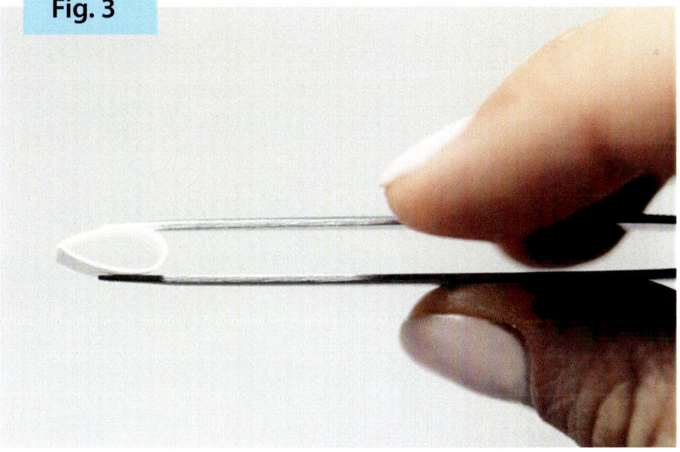

6. Dip the vertical cut edges (**Fig. 4**) and the horizontal bottom edge into the glue. Use tweezers to hold the petal for a couple seconds to adhere the petals to the background and to the flower centers (**Fig. 5**). Glue all the petals to the background.

Fig. 4

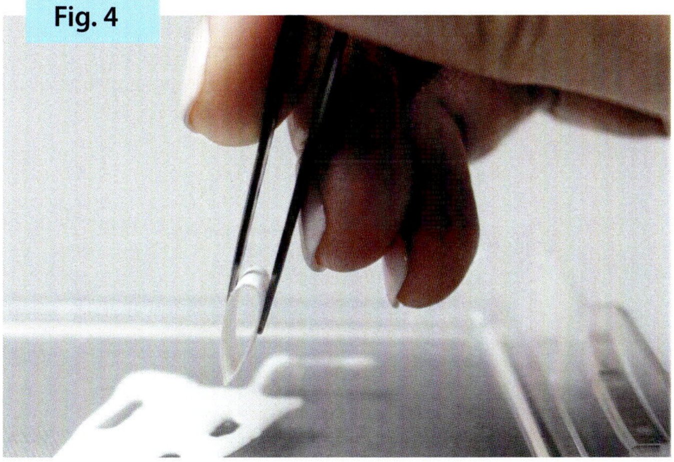

Fig. 5

7. Use green random length paper strips to make stems (**Fig. 6**). Curl the ends of the paper strips slightly in the opposite direction and glue them to the background. Glue the paper strips together in the middle to hold the stems together.

Fig. 6

8. Tie the ribbon into a bow. Glue the bow to the stems. Trim ribbon ends as desired.

9. Place the artwork in the frame if desired.

The Cats are In Love

SHOPPING LIST

- ☐ Paper strips 5-10 mm (¼" to ⅜") wide: black, white, and red
- ☐ 5" x 7" piece of watercolor paper for background
- ☐ 2½" x 7" piece each of white and black cardstock
- ☐ Scissors
- ☐ Tweezers
- ☐ Ruler for measuring
- ☐ Tape for tracing
- ☐ Elmer's® Glue-All® Multi-Purpose Glue Extra Strong Formula
- ☐ Metal embossing stylus (optional)
- ☐ Pencil (optional)
- ☐ Frame with 5" x 7" opening (optional)

Instructions

Note: *Follow* ***Curling****, page 43, to curl each strip before shaping.*

1. For the background, glue black cardstock on the left side of the background and white cardstock on the right side **(Fig. 1)**.
2. Follow **Tracing**, page 42, to transfer pattern, page 34, to the background.
3. For cat's bodies, use white and black 6" paper strips and follow **Hollow Drop**, page 45, to make two Hollow Drops. Glue white cat body on the black background and black cat body on the white background **(Fig. 2)**.

Fig. 1

Fig. 2

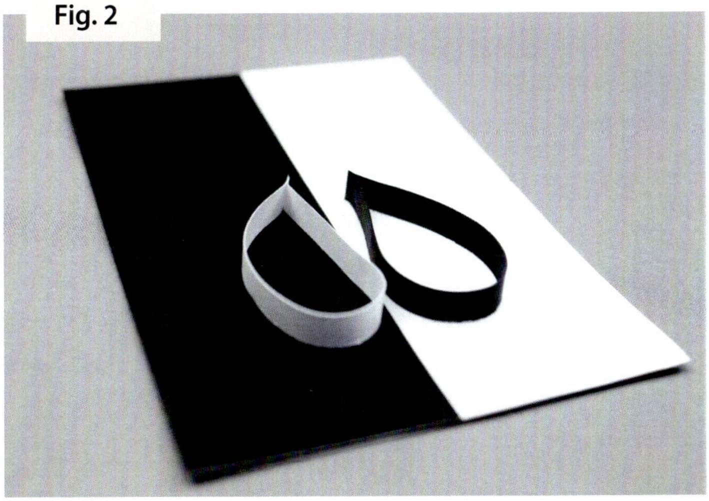

4. Follow **Tear Drop**, page 45, and use a 5½" red paper strip to make a Tear Drop. Make a total of four Tear Drops. Glue 2 Tear Drops together to make a small heart **(Fig. 3)**. Make two small hearts, one for each cat. Glue hearts inside the cat's bodies.

Fig. 3

5. Follow **Open Scroll**, page 44, to use an 11" paper strip, a 5½" paper strip and smaller paper strips to make different sized Open Scrolls from black and white strips. Follow the pattern to fill the bodies (**Fig. 4**).

Fig. 4

6. For heads, follow **Loose Coil**, page 44, and use one black and one white 11" paper strip to make Loose Coils approximately 1" in diameter. Glue the heads to the background (**Fig. 5**).

Fig. 5

7. For tails, use one white and one black 11" paper strip to make two Open Scrolls. Curl tails as desired. Glue them to the background (**Fig. 6**).

Fig. 6

8. For each ear, use 1" paper strip for outer ear and ½" paper strip for inner ear. Fold the pieces of paper in half. Glue the bigger ear first and then glue the smaller one inside the bigger one (**Fig. 7**).

Fig. 7

9. For large heart, use an 11" red paper strip to make a Tear Drop. Make a total of two Tear Drops. Glue Tear Drops together to make a large heart. Glue heart above the cats (**Fig. 8**).

Fig. 8

10. Place the artwork in the frame if desired.

Ice Cream Cactus

Instructions

***Note:** Follow **Curling**, page 43, to curl each strip before shaping.*

1. Follow **Tracing**, page 42, to transfer pattern, page 39, to the background.

2. Follow **Creating an Outline**, page 43, and use brown paper strips to outline the ice cream cone. Glue the outline to the background.

3. For cone bottom, follow **Measuring**, page 44, to cut brown paper strips the necessary length to fit diagonally in one direction across the cone. Glue paper strips to background, leaving ¼" between strips. When gluing, dip all three sides into the glue to adhere the strips properly **(Fig. 1)**.

SHOPPING LIST

- ☐ Paper strips 5-10 mm (¼" to ⅜") wide: brown, pink, green, and yellow
- ☐ 5" x 7" piece of watercolor paper for background
- ☐ Scissors
- ☐ Tweezers
- ☐ Ruler for measuring
- ☐ Tape for tracing
- ☐ Elmer's® Glue-All® Multi-Purpose Glue Extra Strong Formula
- ☐ Metal embossing stylus (optional)
- ☐ Pencil (optional)
- ☐ Frame with 5" x 7" opening (optional)

Fig. 1

4. Measure and arrange each paper strip before gluing to fit diagonally in the opposite direction across the cone **(Fig. 2)**.

Fig. 2

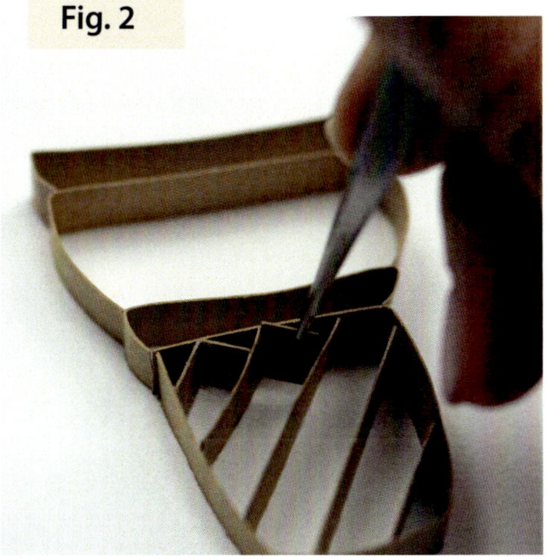

5. To fill top and middle of the ice cream cone, measure horizontally across area and cut as many paper pieces as desired to fill area. Glue pieces to background.

6. To fill last area of ice cream cone, fold brown paper strip approximately every ⅞" to make an accordion shape with 8 sides **(Fig. 3)**. Glue paper strip in area.

Fig. 3

7. Follow **Tight Coil**, page 44, and use a 3" yellow paper strip to make a Tight Coil for the center of the flower. Follow **Tear Drop**, page 45, and use 3" of pink paper strip to make a Tear Drop. Make a total of six Tear Drops to build a flower. Use one 11" paper strip and one 4" paper strip to make two Tight Coils for flower buds. Glue the flower pieces to the background following the pattern **(Fig. 4)**.

Fig. 4

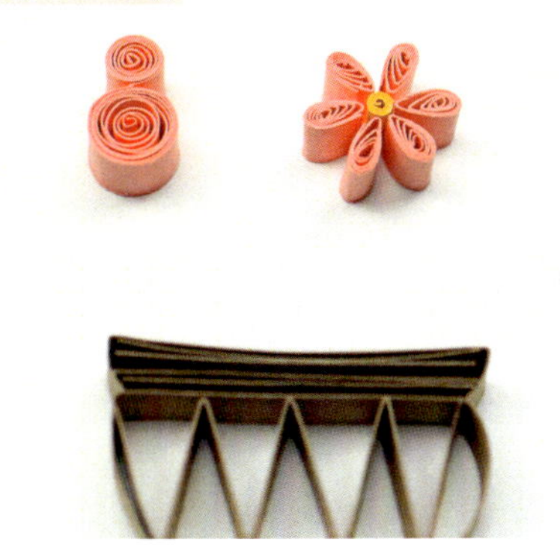

8. Follow **Creating an Outline**, page 43, and use green paper strips to build a cactus outline. Arrange and cut necessary lengths of paper strips before gluing **(Fig. 5)**.

Fig. 5

9. For spines, cut green strips into pieces ¼" or shorter. Glue spines to background in groups of 2 or 3 **(Fig. 6)**.

Fig. 6

10. Place the artwork in the frame if desired.

Floral Heart

SHOPPING LIST

- ☐ Paper strips 5-10 mm (¼" to ⅜") wide: purple, dark purple, hot pink, light pink, and green
- ☐ 5" x 7" piece of watercolor paper for background
- ☐ Scissors
- ☐ Tweezers
- ☐ Ruler for measuring
- ☐ Tape for tracing
- ☐ Elmer's® Glue-All® Multi-Purpose Glue Extra Strong Formula
- ☐ #16 rhinestones (approximately 4mm)
- ☐ Metal embossing stylus (optional)
- ☐ Pencil (optional)
- ☐ Frame with 5" x 7" opening (optional)

Instructions

***Note:** Follow **Curling**, page 43, to curl each strip before shaping.*

1. Follow **Tracing**, page 42, to transfer pattern, page 35, to the background.

2. To make heart, fold an 11" dark purple strip in half. Curl both ends and glue the ends together **(Fig. 1)**.

Fig. 1

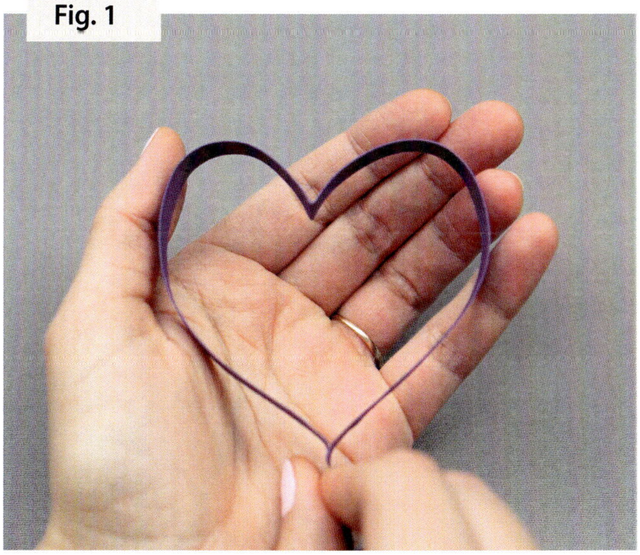

Fig. 2

3. Referring to the pattern, cut a 1" opening from one side of the heart. Glue the heart to the background **(Fig. 2)**.

4. For each flower, cut six 4" paper strips. Follow **Tear Drop**, page 45, to make six Tear Drops. Make a total of 3 purple flowers, 3 pink flowers, and 3 hot pink flowers, adhering them to the background **(Fig. 3)**.

Fig. 3

5. Refer to **Measuring**, page 44, and cut green paper strips to fit between each flower and point of heart. Curl ends of the stems in opposite directions. Glue stems to background **(Fig. 4)**.

Fig. 4

6. Follow **Hollow Drop**, page 45, and use 2"-5" lengths of green paper strips to make Hollow Drops for each leaf. Glue the leaves to the background **(Fig. 5)**.

Fig. 5

7. Using glue and tweezers, adhere 1 rhinestone to the center of each flower **(Fig. 6)**.

Fig. 6

8. Place the artwork in the frame if desired.

Modern Roses

SHOPPING LIST

- ☐ Paper strips 5-10 mm (¼" to ⅜") wide: coral, yellow, ivory, gray, and teal
- ☐ 8" x 8" piece of watercolor paper for background
- ☐ Scissors
- ☐ Tweezers
- ☐ Ruler for measuring
- ☐ Tape for tracing
- ☐ Elmer's® Glue-All® Multi-Purpose Glue Extra Strong Formula
- ☐ Metal embossing stylus (optional)
- ☐ Pencil (optional)
- ☐ Frame with 8" x 8" opening (optional)

Instructions

***Note:** Follow **Curling**, page 43, to curl each strip before shaping.*

1. Follow **Tracing**, page 42, to transfer pattern, page 36, to the background, transferring outer triangles if desired to add more geometric details.

2. Follow **Open Scroll**, page 44, and use a 3" coral paper strip to make an Open Scroll for the center of the large rose. Glue the Open Scroll in the center of the large rose (**Fig. 1**).

Fig. 1

3. For large rose petals, cut ten to thirteen 1" coral paper strips. Curl each strip with your fingers as if dividing it into two parts (**Fig. 2**). Try not to make each strip the same. The rose will look more natural if the strips are curled differently.

Fig. 2

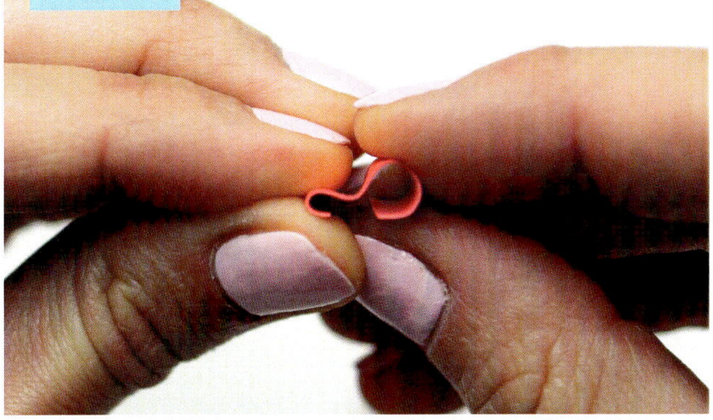

4. Arrange the petals on the background, repositioning the strips until you are happy with the way it looks **(Fig. 3)**. Glue the petals around the Open Scroll center in a circle to create a rose. Continue with 1½" coral paper strips to make and glue more petals for the rose.

5. Make two small roses in the same way using 2" yellow paper strips for the center of the roses and 1" yellow paper strips for the petals **(Fig. 4)**.

Fig. 3

Fig. 4

6. Use 3", 2", and 1" green paper strips to make a variety of leaves. Fold the strip in half and turn the edge with pencil or a stylus to curl both halves. Apply some glue to the end of one side. Adhere both sides together using fingers or a pair of tweezers to hold them to get an almond shape. Glue the leaves to the background **(Fig. 5)**.

Fig. 5

7. Add leaf veins using green random sized paper strips **(Fig. 6)**.

Fig. 6

8. If desired, follow **Measuring**, page 44, to create a triangle outline with gray paper strips following the pattern **(Fig. 7)**.

Fig. 7

9. Follow **Tight Coil**, page 44, and use 1" ivory paper strips to make a total of 13 Tight Coils to build lines at the bottom of the design; glue to background. Follow **Hollow Drop**, page 45, and use 1" ivory paper strips to make 3 Hollow Drops. Glue Hollow Drops to background **(Fig. 8)**.

Fig. 8

Fig. 9

10. Use 2" ivory paper strips to make ten Tight Coils and glue to background in a circle on the top of the triangle **(Fig. 9)**.

11. Place the artwork in the frame if desired.

Dolphin & Waves

SHOPPING LIST

- ☐ Paper strips 5-10 mm (¼" to ⅜") wide: baby blue, light blue, and indigo
- ☐ 5" x 7" piece of watercolor paper for background
- ☐ Scissors
- ☐ Tweezers
- ☐ Ruler for measuring
- ☐ Tape for tracing
- ☐ Elmer's® Glue-All® Multi-Purpose Glue Extra Strong Formula
- ☐ Metal embossing stylus (optional)
- ☐ Pencil (optional)
- ☐ Frame with 5" x 7" opening (optional)

Instructions

***Note:** Follow **Curling**, page 43, to curl each strip before shaping.*

1. Follow **Tracing**, page 42, to transfer pattern, page 39, to the background. If you would like a swirlier dolphin, transfer the Open Scrolls inside the dolphin's body.

2. Follow **Creating an Outline**, page 43, to use baby blue paper strips to outline the dolphin body, leaving a space for the fin **(Fig. 1)**. Glue the strips to the background.

Fig. 1

3. Use baby blue paper strips to make outline of fins and tail and glue them to the background **(Fig. 2)**.

Fig. 2

4. Follow **Double Scroll**, page 45, and use one 11" light blue paper strip and one 11" indigo paper strip to make a Double Scroll. Make a total of two Double Scrolls and glue one to each side of the dolphin to create waves (**Fig. 3**).

Fig. 3

5. Follow **Open Scroll**, page 44, to add waves using desired length light blue and indigo paper strips and the pattern (**Fig. 4**).

Fig. 4

6. You can stop here and place your artwork into the frame, if desired, or add more Open Scrolls inside the dolphin's body (**Fig. 5**) using baby blue and light blue paper strips. Glue the Open Scrolls to the background following the pattern.

Fig. 5

7. Follow **Loose Coil**, page 44, to make a Loose Coil using a 2" light blue paper strip to fill the nose tip. Use random length paper strips of different colors to finish the dolphin's body. Use baby blue and light blue to make Double Scrolls for the dolphin's tail (**Fig. 6**). Glue all pieces to the background.

Fig. 6

8. Place the artwork in the frame if desired.

Whale Tail

SHOPPING LIST

- ☐ Paper strips 5-10 mm (¼" to ⅜") wide: white, purple, light blue, blue, green, yellow, orange, and red
- ☐ 5" x 7" piece of watercolor paper for background
- ☐ Scissors
- ☐ Tweezers
- ☐ Ruler for measuring
- ☐ Tape for tracing
- ☐ Elmer's® Glue-All® Multi-Purpose Glue Extra Strong Formula
- ☐ Metal embossing stylus (optional)
- ☐ Pencil (optional)
- ☐ Frame with 5" x 7" opening (optional)

Instructions

Note: *Follow **Curling**, page 43, to curl each strip before shaping.*

1. Follow **Tracing**, page 42, to transfer pattern, page 37, to the background.

2. Follow **Creating an Outline**, page 43, and use white paper strips to outline the whale tail. Glue strips to background (**Fig. 1**).

Fig. 1

3. For waves, cut 4" light blue and blue paper strips. Curl both ends of paper strips in opposite directions and glue them to the background (**Fig. 2**).

Fig. 2

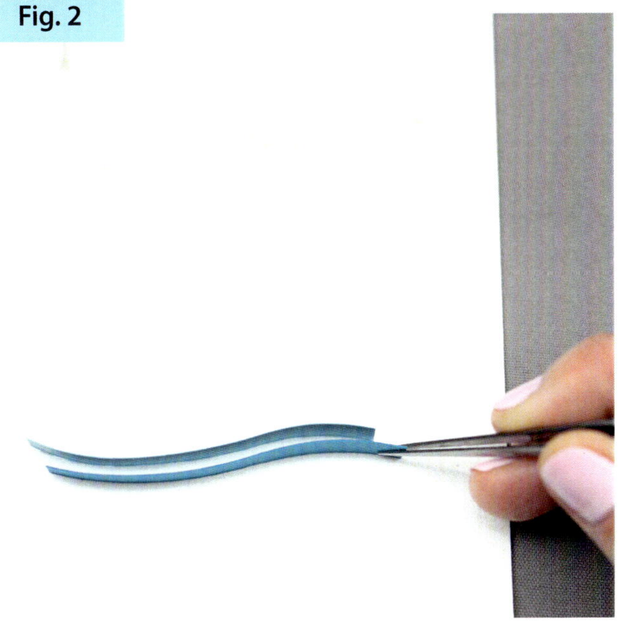

4. Follow **Measuring**, page 44, to cut white paper strips to divide the outline into triangles **(Fig. 3)**. Glue the paper strips to the background **(Fig. 4)**.

Fig. 3

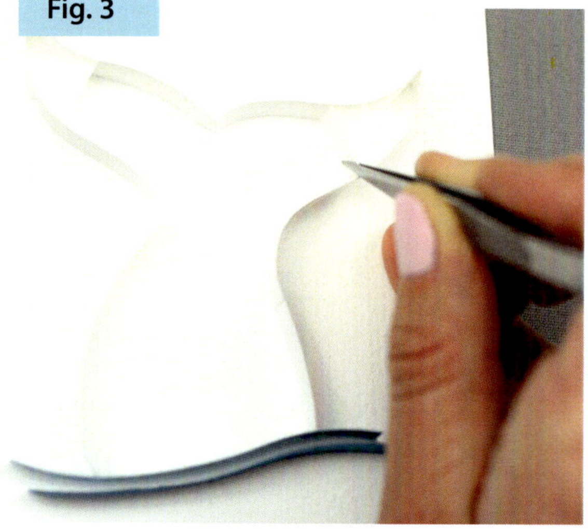

Fig. 4

5. For each large triangle, follow **Open Scroll**, page 44, and use a 5" – 6" strip to make one Open Scroll. Follow **Loose Coil**, page 44, and use 2" – 4" strips to make 2 matching color Loose Coils. The size depends on the triangle size. The bigger the Scroll or Coil, the longer the paper strip you will need. Glue scroll and coils to background (**Fig. 5**). Repeat to fill each triangle with quilling shape using the pattern.

Fig. 5

6. For the triangles in the tips of the tail, use a 5" – 6" strip to make an Open Scroll. Use a matching color 5" – 6" strip to make a Loose Coil. Glue the scroll and coil to the background (**Fig. 6**).

Fig. 6

7. Place the artwork in the frame if desired.

Floral Elephant

SHOPPING LIST

- ☐ Paper strips 5-10 mm (¼" to ⅜") wide: gray, light pink, lilac, green, and yellow
- ☐ 5" x 7" piece of watercolor paper for background
- ☐ Scissors
- ☐ Tweezers
- ☐ Ruler for measuring
- ☐ Tape for tracing
- ☐ Elmer's® Glue-All® Multi-Purpose Glue Extra Strong Formula
- ☐ #16 rhinestones (approximately 4mm)
- ☐ Metal embossing stylus (optional)
- ☐ Pencil (optional)
- ☐ Frame with 5" x 7" opening (optional)

Instructions

***Note:** Follow **Curling**, page 43, to curl each strip before shaping.*

1. Follow **Tracing**, page 42, to transfer pattern, page 35, to the background.

2. Follow **Creating an Outline**, page 43, and use gray paper strips to outline the elephant. Glue the pieces to the background **(Fig. 1)**.

3. Follow **Hollow Drop**, page 45, and use 1½" paper strips to make large petals and 1" paper strips to make small petals to fill elephant's body. Make six small lilac petals, six light pink small petals, six light pink large petals, 9 yellow small petals, and three large yellow petals.

4. Use the pattern to place the petals. Using tweezers, dip two sides, a horizontal bottom edge, and a vertical edge into the glue and adhere the petals into the elephant's outline. Hold it for a couple seconds to adhere the petals to the background **(Fig. 2)**.

Fig. 1

Fig. 2

5. For the stems of the flowers, follow **Open Scroll**, page 44, and use green random size paper strips to make Open Scrolls. Glue Open Scrolls to background **(Fig. 3)**.

Fig. 3

6. For leaves, use a 1" green paper strip to make a **Hollow Drop**. Continue with 1" green paper strips making Hollow Drops. Pinch each Hollow Drop to make a leaf **(Fig. 4)**.

Fig. 4

7. Glue the leaves close to the stems and fill the rest of the space with leaves **(Fig. 5)**.

Fig. 5

8. For flower, make six **Hollow Drops** to make petals. Glue the petals to the background above and to the left of the elephant's trunk. Follow **Measuring**, page 44, to cut stems. Glue a green stem from the flower to the trunk and another green stem from the trunk to the right. Make one Open Scroll with desired length of green paper and glue it to the stem **(Fig. 6)**.

Fig. 6

9. Using glue and tweezers, adhere 1 rhinestone to the center of each flower **(Fig. 7)**.

10. Place the artwork in the frame if desired.

Fig. 7

The Quilled Mandala

SHOPPING LIST

- ☐ Paper strips 5-10 mm (¼" to ⅜") wide: peach, teal, and yellow
- ☐ 9" x 9" piece of watercolor paper for background
- ☐ Scissors
- ☐ Tweezers
- ☐ Ruler for measuring
- ☐ Tape for tracing
- ☐ Elmer's® Glue-All® Multi-Purpose Glue Extra Strong Formula
- ☐ Metal embossing stylus (optional)
- ☐ Pencil (optional)
- ☐ Frame with 9" x 9" opening (optional)

Instructions

*Note: Follow **Curling**, page 43, to curl each strip before shaping.*

1. Follow **Tracing**, page 42, to transfer pattern, page 38, to the background.

2. Adhere two 11" peach paper strips together end to end (**Fig. 1**); allow to dry a few minutes.

Fig. 1

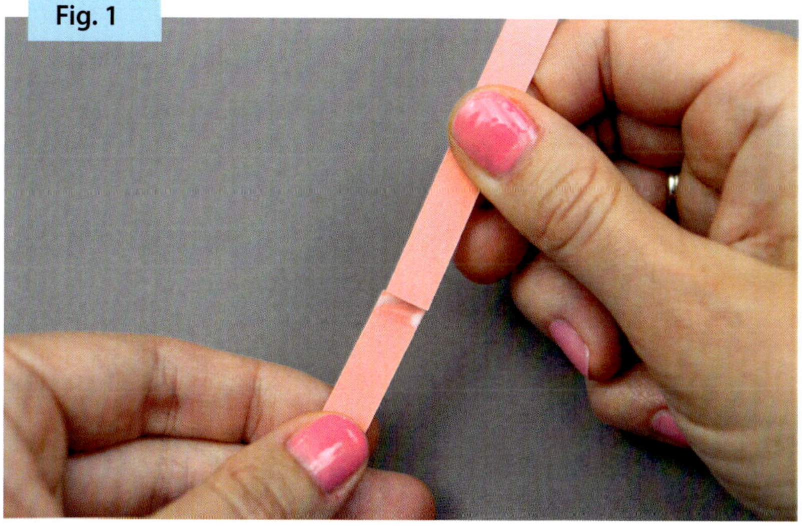

3. Following **Open Scroll**, page 44, use the long strip to make an Open Scroll with a coil 1" in diameter. Curl the end of the strip in the opposite direction of the coil (**Fig. 2**).

Fig. 2

4. Repeat Steps 2-3 to make eight Open Scrolls. Glue them together on the background using the pattern and matching the ends in the center (**Fig. 3**).

Fig. 3

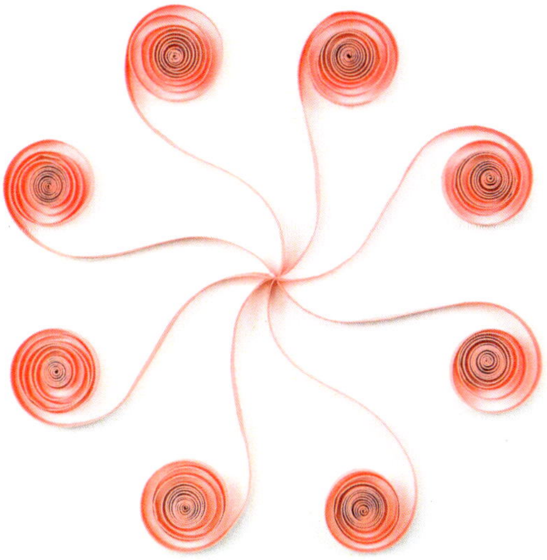

5. Using one 11" teal paper strip, make a 5/8" diameter Open Scroll. Make a total of eight Open Scrolls and glue them to the background beginning in the center **(Fig. 4)**. The teal Open Coil should be glued in the opposite direction from the peach Open Coil. Leave some space between the end of the peach and teal Open Scrolls to insert other pieces.

Fig. 4

6. Follow **Hollow Drop**, page 45, and use 4" yellow paper strips to make a total of 24 Hollow Drops (3 pieces for each mandala section). Holding the end of the Hollow Drop, wrap the ends of the paper strip around a stylus or pencil about halfway to the end **(Fig. 5)**.

Fig. 5

7. Glue groups of 3 yellow Hollow Drops between the teal and peach Open Scrolls in each mandala section **(Fig. 6)**.

Fig. 6

8. Use a 5½" long teal paper strip to make an Open Scroll approximately 3/8" in diameter and 4" teal paper strips to make two Open Scrolls approximately 5/16" in diameter. Glue the larger teal Open Scroll to the peach strip 2" from the center of the mandala **(Fig. 7)**.

Fig. 7

TIP:
When working with symmetrical projects always assemble shapes from the center of the pattern and work your way out toward the pattern's edge. Try to make the same size shapes each time.

Fig. 8

Fig. 9

9. Add the smaller Open Scrolls to the left and to the right of the larger teal scroll (**Fig. 8**).

10. Repeat Steps 8 – 9 to fill all mandala sections.

11. Following **Tight Coils**, page 44, use 2" and 1" peach paper strips to make Tight Coils and glue them near the center for each mandala section. Glue the smaller Tight Coil closer to the center and the larger Tight Coil further from the center (**Fig. 9**).

12. Use 4", 3", and 2" yellow paper strips to make ¼", 3⁄16", and ⅛" diameter Loose Coils for each mandala section. Glue the Loose Coils to the background with largest coil closer to the inside and smallest coil closer to the outside (**Fig. 10**).

13. Place the artwork in the frame if desired.

Fig. 10

Coffee

SHOPPING LIST

- ☐ Paper strips 5-10 mm (¼" to ⅜") wide: ivory and brown
- ☐ 5" x 7" piece of watercolor paper for background
- ☐ Scissors
- ☐ Tweezers
- ☐ Ruler for measuring
- ☐ Tape for tracing
- ☐ Elmer's® Glue-All® Multi-Purpose Glue Extra Strong Formula
- ☐ Metal embossing stylus (optional)
- ☐ Pencil (optional)
- ☐ Frame with 5" x 7" opening (optional)

Instructions

***Note:** Follow **Curling**, page 43, to curl each strip before shaping.*

1. Follow **Tracing**, page 42, to transfer pattern, page 37, to the background.

2. Follow **Creating an Outline**, page 43, and use ivory paper strips to make the cup outline. Glue the strips to the background **(Fig. 1)**.

3. Follow **Open Scroll**, page 44, to make an Open Scroll using one 11" ivory paper strip. Glue it on the right side of the cup to make the handle of the cup **(Fig. 2)**.

Fig. 1

Fig. 2

4. For coffee, use an approximately 4½" long brown paper strip to make an almond shape to fill top part of cup. Make at least four almond shapes, each smaller than the previous one. Glue pieces to background **(Fig. 3)**.

Fig. 3

5. When a thin space is left, follow **Measuring**, page 44, and cut a brown paper strip the necessary length. Glue the strip in the middle of the last almond **(Fig. 4)**.

Fig. 4

6. Use one 11" ivory paper strip to make an Open Scroll. Make a total of three Open Scrolls. Glue the scrolls on the background following the pattern **(Fig. 5)**.

Fig. 5

7. Make at least five more ivory smaller Open Scrolls to fill the cup. Glue the scrolls to the background **(Fig. 6)**.

Fig. 6

8. Use one 11" brown paper strip and a 5½" paper strip to make two Open Scrolls in the shape of the letter "f". Using a pencil or a stylus, curl the end of the strip in the opposite direction of the scroll **(Fig. 7)**.

Fig. 7

9. Follow **Loose Coil**, page 44, and use a 5½" brown paper strip to make a Loose Coil in the shape of a letter "o". Use a 5½" ivory paper strip to make an Open Scroll in the shape of the letter "C". Use a 2" ivory paper strip to make an additional Open Scroll for the bottom of the "C". Use 2" of ivory and brown paper strips to make two letters "e" (**Fig. 8**).

Fig. 8

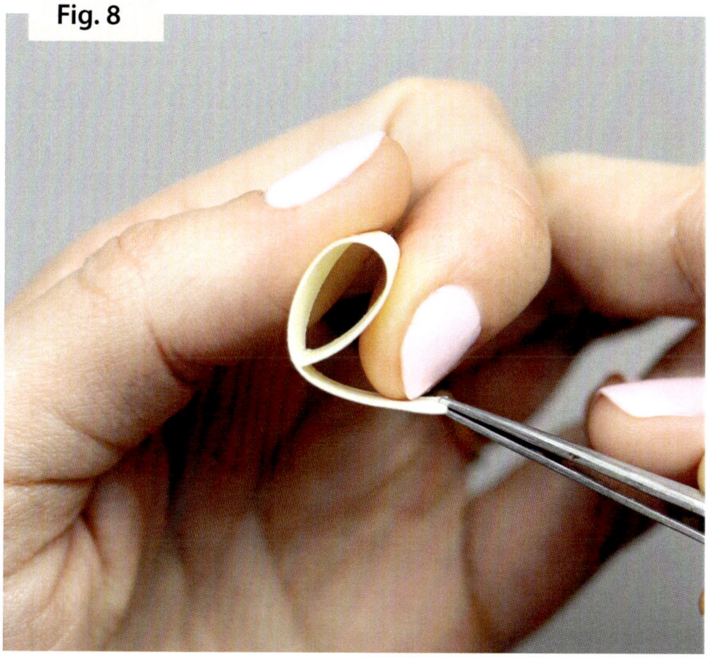

10. Glue letters "f" first, starting from the middle of the cup. Continue with the letter "o" and glue it to the left of the big "f" and the brown "e" to the right of small letter "f". Finish with the letter "C" to the left of the letter "o" and ivory letter "e" to the right from brown letter "e" (**Fig. 9**).

Fig. 9

11. Place the artwork in the frame if desired.

Patterns

THE CATS ARE IN LOVE

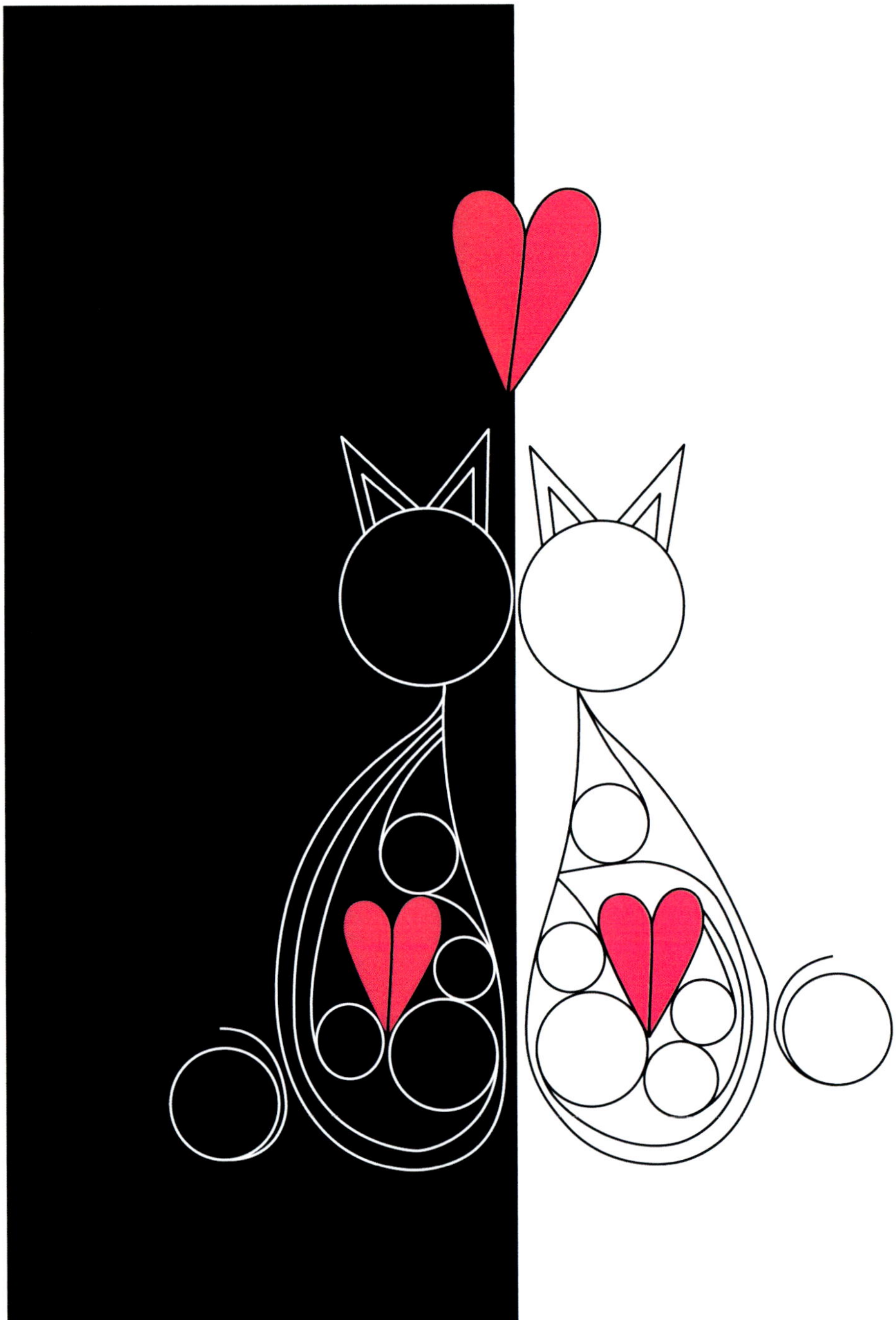

MODERN ROSES

THE QUILLED MANDALA

General Instructions

MATERIALS AND TOOLS

Quilling Paper and Quilling Paper Strips

When choosing paper for quilling you can use precut quilling paper strips or you can cut strips yourself from quilling paper. The most important thing when buying quilling paper strips or quilling paper is to choose the correct weight. Usually it is 120-190 GSM (grams per square meter). If the paper is too thin it will not hold its shape. When you roll a coil it should stay in that shape and glue easily to the background.

Quilling paper strips come in a wide variety of colors and widths. I have found that the most popular width for beginners is 5 mm. I recommend using 5, 7, or 10 mm paper strips for quilling projects. The wider the strips you use the more beautiful your project looks. Quilling paper strips also come in a variety of lengths. I used 10 mm wide and 11" long paper strips in all my projects in this book.

I cut my paper strips myself using 8½" x 11" pieces of 65 lb (175 GSM) weight cardstock with a ruler and utility knife. Also, the paper can be cut with a paper trimmer. If you decide to cut your own paper strips using scissors or a utility knife, you'll need a ruler and pencil to help measure. Make sure to use a cutting mat to protect the surface underneath if using a utility knife. If you use a paper trimmer, decide what width you'd like for your paper strips and measure those using the ruler on the paper trimmer. Using a paper trimmer will produce strips much faster than using scissors or a utility knife. I usually cut my paper strips ¼" to ⅜" wide.

Both precut and hand cut strips have a front and back side. At first glance it is difficult to determine which one is which. The front side of the strip rounds slightly to the back and has a rougher surface. The back side has a smoother surface.

For your first projects you can use any type of color paper you have at home. Just be aware that printer paper and construction paper will fade faster than quilling paper strips or quilling paper. Keep your artwork away from sunlight.

Scissors

You will need scissors with sharp blades for cutting paper strips. Also, you can use scissors to cut a background of the indicated size.

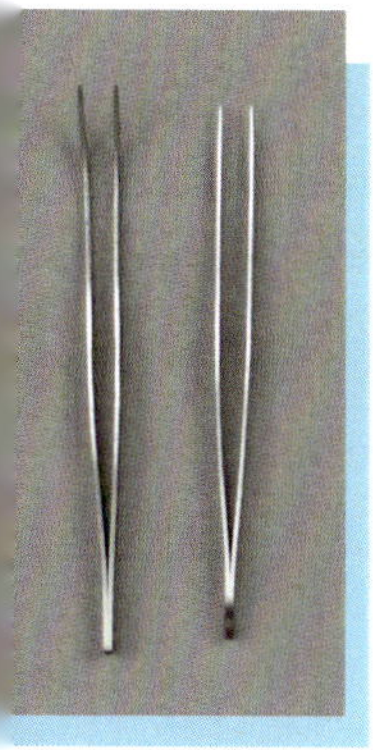

Tweezers

Tweezers help to hold the pieces and place them onto the background. The rolled pieces can be rather small and delicate so it's best to use a nice pair of tweezers to hold them while you work. Any regular pair of tweezers will do, as paper quilling does not require a unique tool for this process.

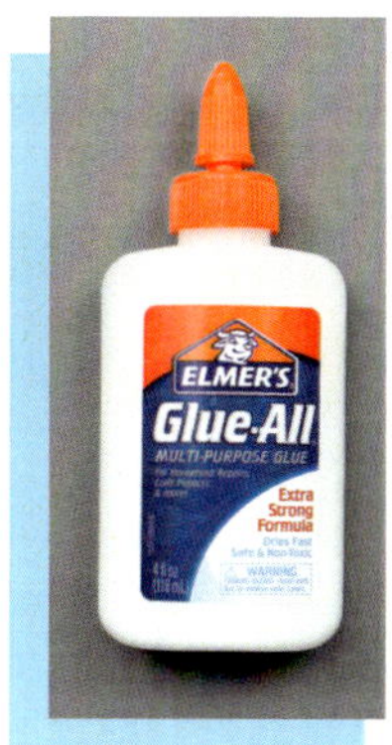

Glue

You can find a variety of glues on the market. The most important properties of the glue for quilling are transparency and adhesion. White glue dries clear and is therefore invisible. The most popular and easy to find is Elmer's® Glue-All® Multi-Purpose Glue Extra Strong Formula. It is water-based and thicker than regular school glue, fast drying, and has a strong bond.

The glue is generally used twice in paper quilling: first to secure the shape of the rolled paper and second to adhere the shape onto the background.

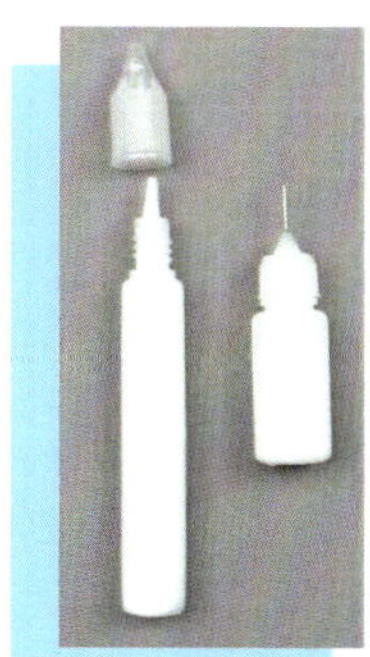

TIP:

Use craft glue in a bottle with a precision tip to help you place the glue in the correct spots.

Ruler

A ruler is an indispensable tool in quilling projects. It is used for measuring how long each strip of paper should be. Also, it helps to measure the diameter of a coil if needed.

Tape

Clear tape is used for taping your pattern and watercolor paper together for transferring the pattern. Before adhering, touch the sticky side of the tape several times with your fingers so it is not so sticky. This will assure the tape does not damage the watercolor paper.

Cutting Mat

A self-healing mat is needed if you are going to cut your own paper strips to protect the surface of your table from scratches and cuts. It also protects your table when gluing.

Watercolor Paper

For each project you need a background on which to place your quilling pieces. I used 300 GSM watercolor paper. It is easy to find at any craft store.

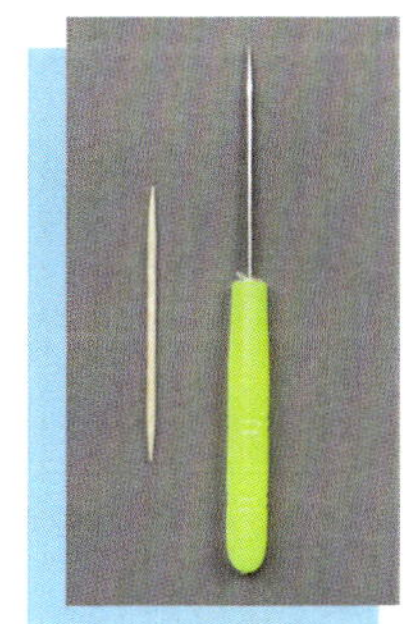

Needle Tool or Toothpick

Use a needle tool or toothpick to help you rolling the paper strips. The toothpicks also come in handy for applying liquid glue.

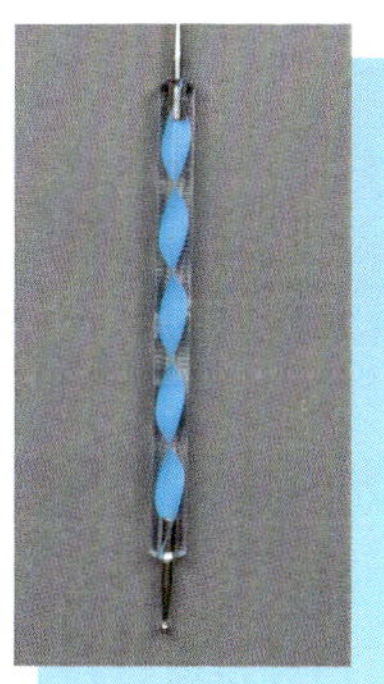

Metal Embossing Stylus

A metal embossing stylus is very helpful to curl your paper strips in the desire way to avoid paper cuts. Also, a stylus can also be used to trace the pattern on the background. I use it all the time in quilling projects.

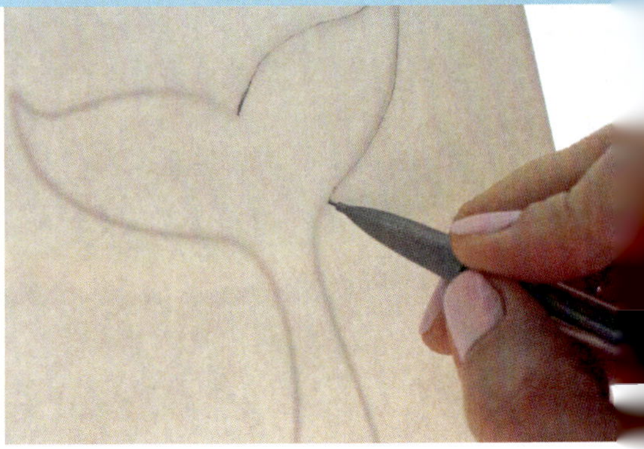

Tracing

Tracing with pencil. Place the pattern **under** your watercolor paper background, securing the layers with tape. Use a light table or sunny window to trace the pattern, pressing lightly on the pencil to leave a barely visible line. Don't forget to erase the pencil line after you make your quilling paper shape and before gluing.

Tracing with Stylus, needle tool, or toothpick. Place the pattern on **top of** the watercolor paper background, securing the layers with tape. Trace the pattern, pressing lightly on the tool to leave a barely visible outline on your background.

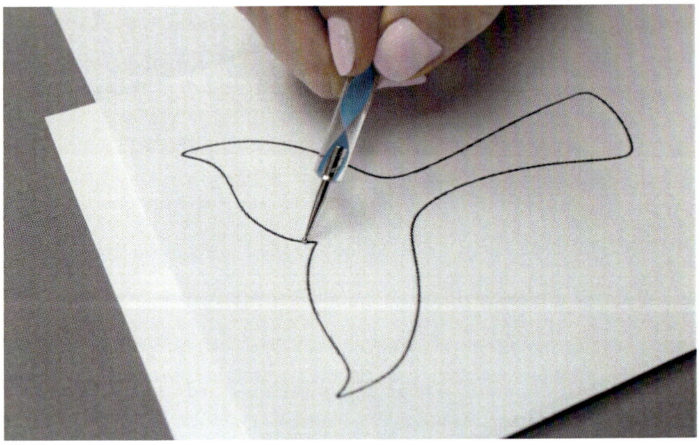

TIP:
You also can print out or draw your own pattern for new designs.

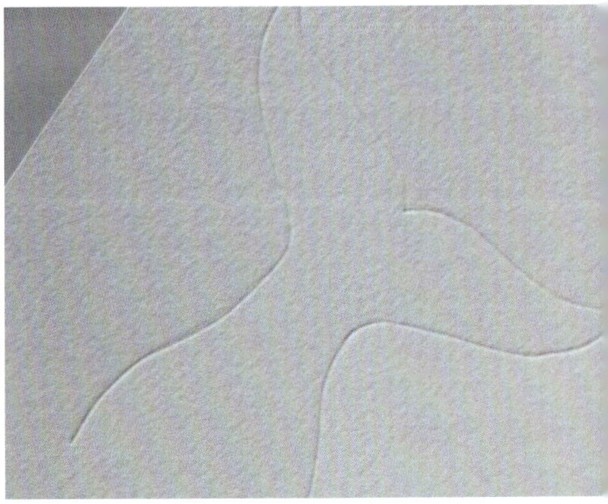

Frames

Quilling can be framed just like any other artwork, with a little extra care when choosing just what type of frame you use.

Quilling paper art is 3D and has more height to it than photographs or painted artwork. There is a chance that the rolled paper strips may get squished in a frame with glass. Below are some recommendations for framing paper quilling.

Option №1. Frame your quilling artwork without glass! This option will allow you to have the most choices in frames. There are two disadvantages with this method. Your artwork is not safe from dust and will fade faster.

Option №2. A shadowbox. With a shadowbox there is a 2" or larger gap between the back of the frame and the glass. A benefit of using a shadowbox for your quilling is that there will be plenty of room between the back of the frame and the glass. They save your artwork from dust and protect from sunlight.

In both options you can use a picture frame mat. Mats tend to lend a more complete look to the artwork and they also draw the viewers eye in towards the center of the frame, right to your beautiful quilling paper art.

Curling

Before using each shaped paper strip, use a stylus, pencil, or your fingers to curve the paper strip. Gently pull the length of the paper strip over the tool to curl the strip slightly. This helps avoid a kink in the paper strip when you roll it and gives a curve to the paper strip. This is not necessary for a strip that will remain straight.

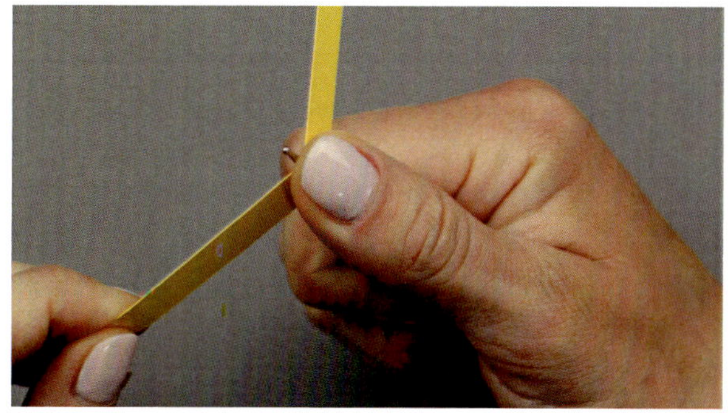

Creating an Outline

Most of the projects follow **Tracing**, page 42, to create an outline using a pattern which is filled with different quilling shapes. You can fill it with different coils, scrolls, and drops. Follow the steps below using the whale tail pattern as a guide.

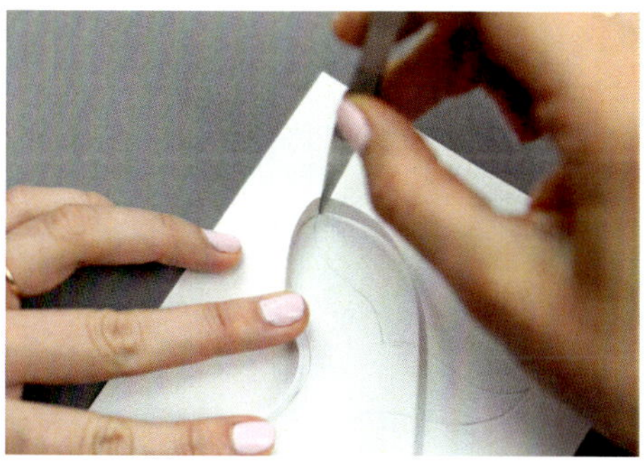

Follow **Curling** to curl each strip as needed along the pattern. Place the strip on top of the pattern. When a fold is needed, use a pair of tweezers to mark the point on the outline where it should be folded.

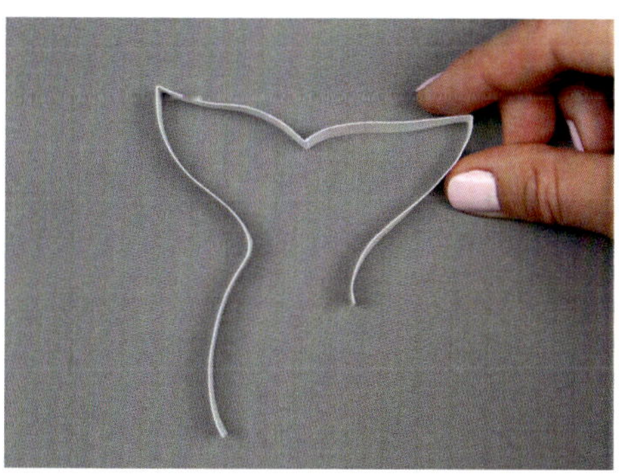

Fold the strip where you have made the mark with the tweezers, ensuring the fold is perpendicular to the edge of the strip and straight. If the fold is not made carefully here, you will encounter problems gluing later. Continue to shape the remaining part of the outline in the same way.

I will repeatedly pick the piece up and place it on the pattern, comparing, back and forth, until I have the right shape. Once the piece is shaped to match the pattern, don't forget to erase the pencil, if used. Then I will finally glue it to the background.

Sometimes one strip is not enough to finish the outline. Follow **Measuring**, page 44, to measure the necessary lengths to make the rest of the outline; overlap the ends and glue to add it to your existing outline.

Sometimes it's necessary to curl a small piece of paper strip. To do so, wrap the strip around the stylus or pencil and apply pressure. You'll see the strip start to curl.

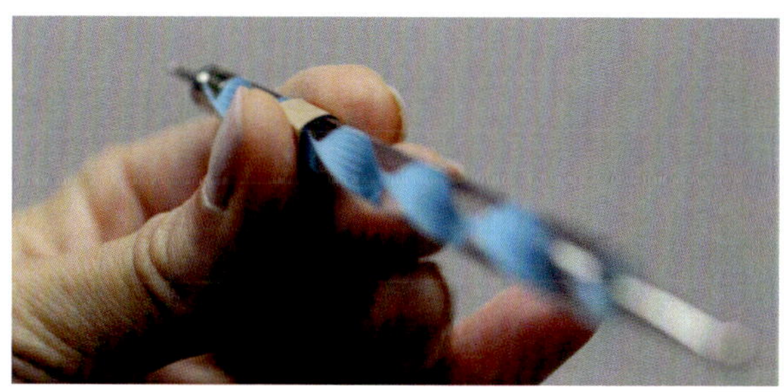

TIP:

To fill the outline with shapes, start in order with the largest shapes to smallest shapes.

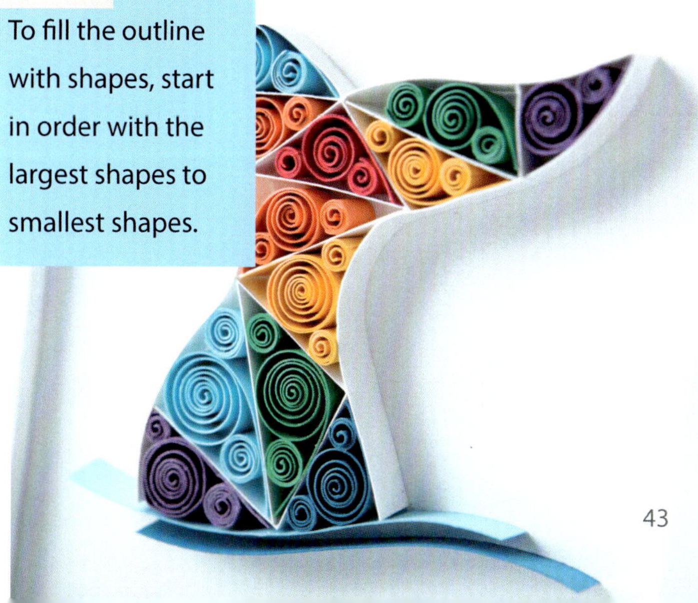

Measuring

Use a ruler to measure the length of paper strip you need to make a shape and a pair of scissors to cut it.

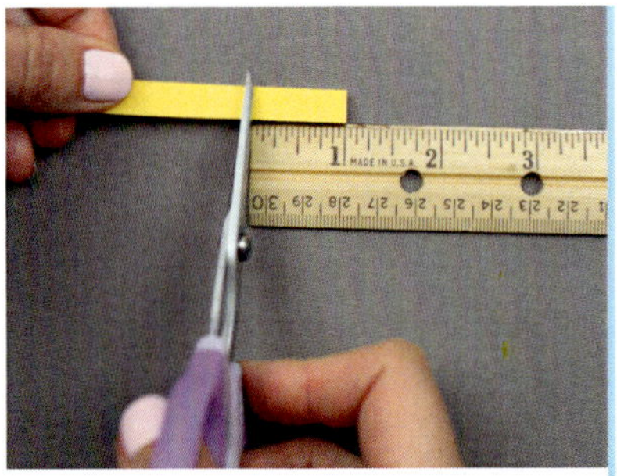

Use a ruler to check the size of a coil.

TIP:

To make consistent size coils, you can use a circle template. With practice, you'll get so good at making coils that you may not need a template at all.

To measure the length of the paper strip you need to glue inside the outline, take a paper strip, place it on the outline and use your finger to mark the point where you need to cut.

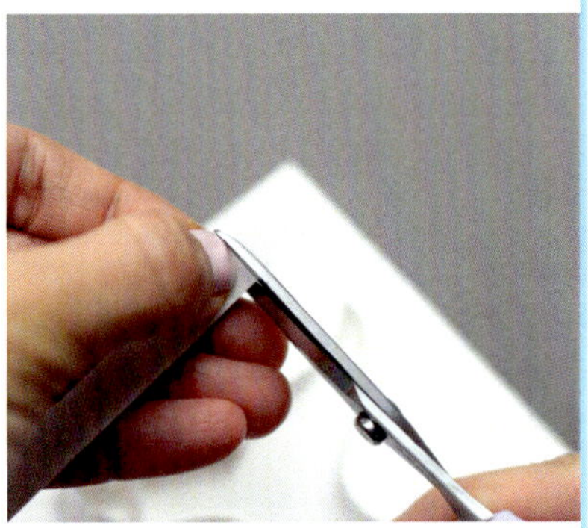

Use scissors to cut the length you have marked.

Place the piece of paper before gluing it. If it is too long, trim it a bit more and place it again. Then glue the paper strip inside the outline.

Creating Shapes

The most frequent process in quilling is making quilled shapes. Here, I explain how to make the shapes used in this book. These are my favorite basic shapes. The rest depends on your imagination and creativity.

Tight Coil

Put the paper strip with the back side up and fold the strip with a needle tool, toothpick, or your fingers, to make 1-1½ turns.

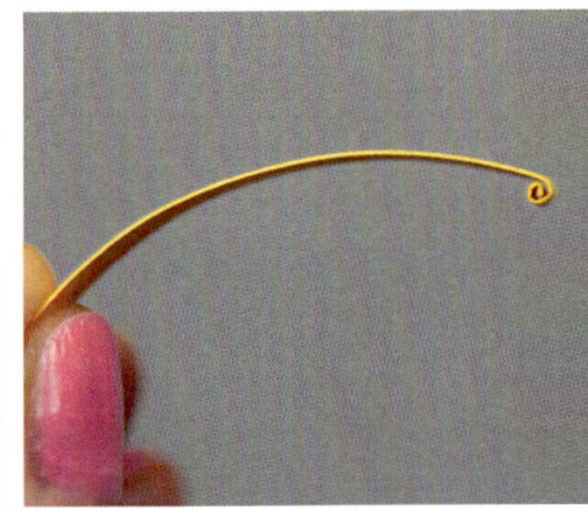

Start to roll the strip using your thumb and index finger. Roll the strip tightly into a "Tight Coil". Glue the end of the paper strip.

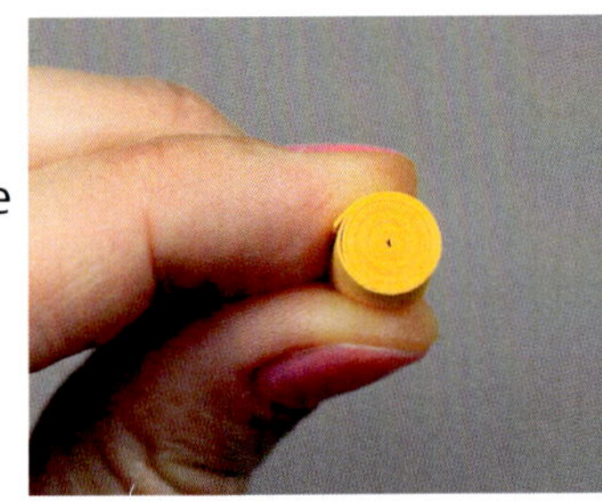

Open Scroll

To make an Open Scroll, make a Tight Coil. Place the Tight Coil on the cushion of the index finger and allow coil to expand. Do not glue the end of the paper strip.

Loosen the Open Scroll to get a larger Open Scroll.

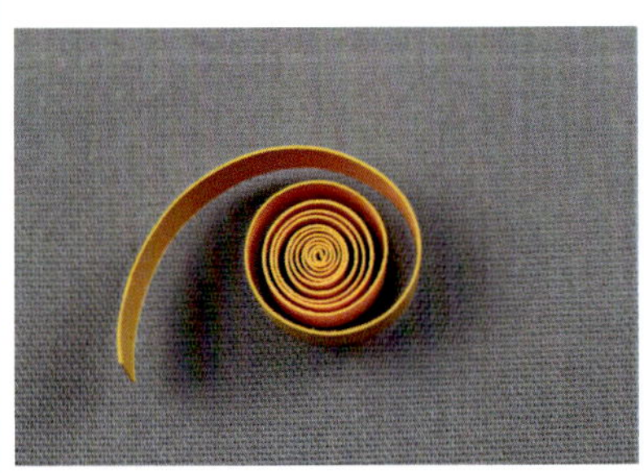

Loose Coil

Make an Open Scroll; loosen the scroll and glue the loose end to get a Loose Coil.

Tear Drop

Make a Loose Coil. Pull the center of the coil with the fingers of your non-dominant hand. With your dominant hand, pinch the opposite side of the Loose Coil along the entire length of the shape. Glue the end of the paper strip.

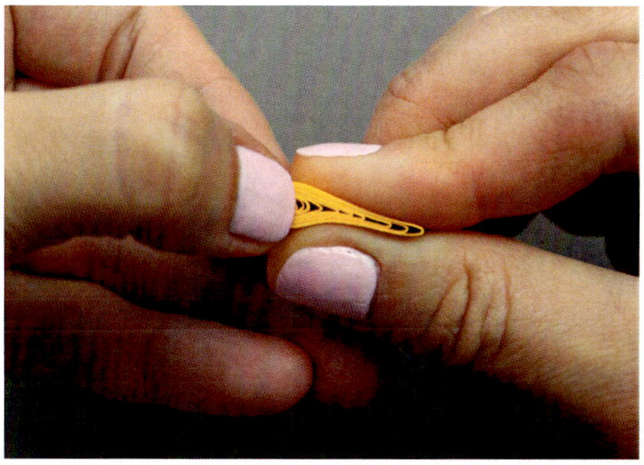

Hollow Drop

Follow **Curling**, page 43, and curl each end of the strip in the same direction with a stylus or pencil. Apply some glue to one end.

Adhere both sides together using fingers or a pair of tweezers to hold them to make a Hollow Drop.

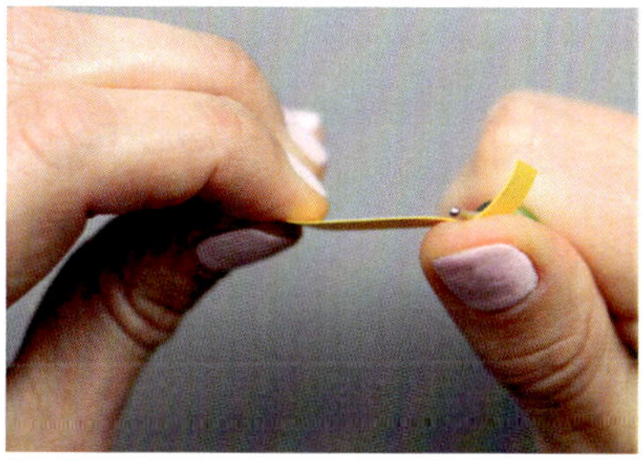

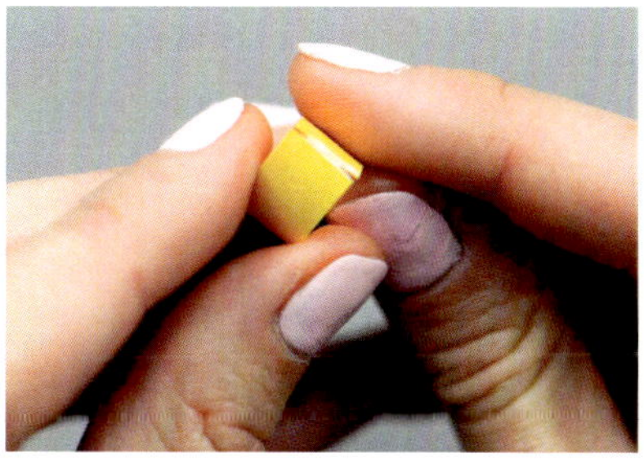

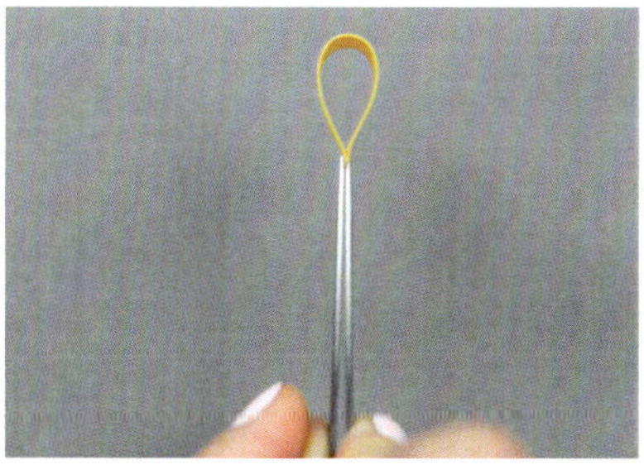

Double Scroll

Glue two paper strips of different colors together.

Make an Open Scroll and pull each strip slightly to open the space between each strip in the coil to make a nice Double Scroll. If you pull too much and are unhappy with how your Open Scroll looks, push the strip back towards the coil end a bit.

Cut any excess paper off and glue the ends of paper strips together.

TIP:

You can use even more than two colors to get a multicolor Scroll.

Gluing

To apply glue, first squeeze some glue into a small container or lid (I usually use the lid from a craft container) or onto a small piece of paper.

Dip the tip of a toothpick into the glue and apply a tiny amount of glue to the strip of quilling paper.

To glue your paper strips or shapes onto the background, use tweezers to dip it right in the glue and glue it to the background.

TIP:

Before starting to glue shapes to the background, arrange the shapes first to make sure the sizes are right and you like how the shapes look on your project.

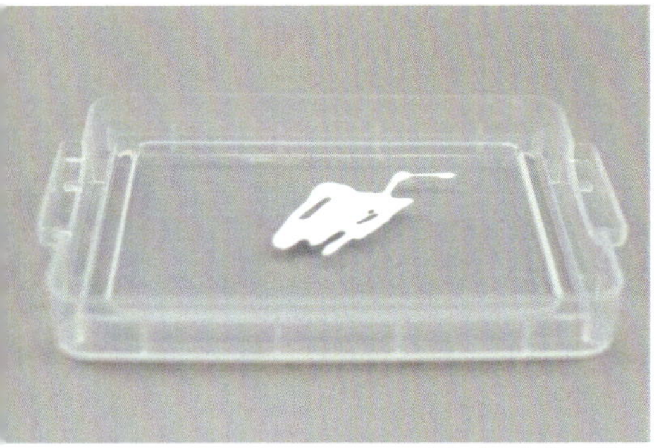

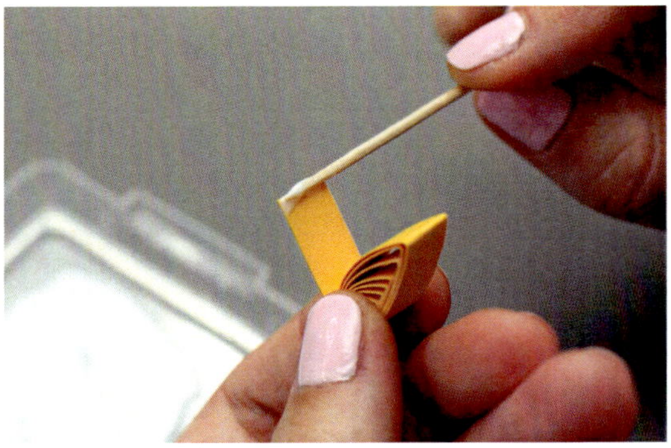

Sometimes it can be easy to apply too much glue to your quilling strip and the glue may be seen on your finished project.

If this happens, use a piece of plastic or another piece of cardstock to flatten the puddle. This way the depth of your glue puddle is very shallow.

This allows you to gently press the quilling shapes into the glue, coating only the edge.

For larger quilling shapes, apply glue directly to the back with a precision tip glue bottle.

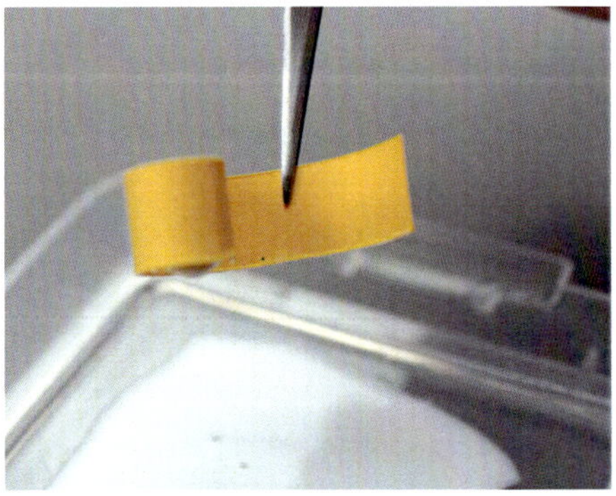

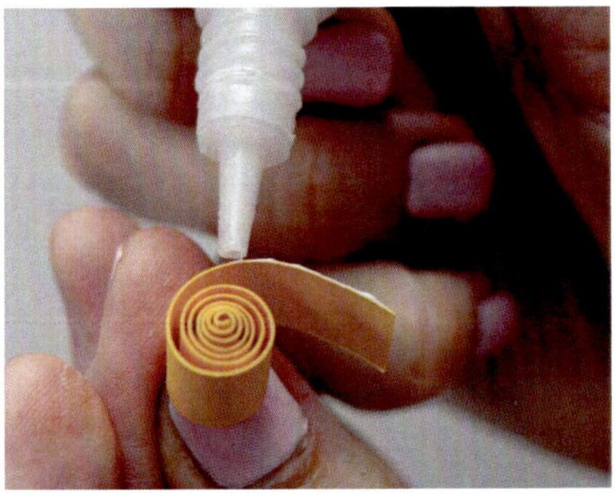

TIP:

Never use more glue than necessary. You want to keep your artwork clean and professional. It's a good idea to keep a small clean paintbrush handy. You can use it to wipe away any glue that seeps out from under your quilling paper once it's on the background.

Meet

ALYONA KOCHUBEY

"To become really good at anything,
you have to practice and repeat,
practice and repeat
until the technique becomes intuitive."

– Paulo Coelho

Alyona Kochubey started paper art several years ago when she wanted to make a birthday card for her daughter's teacher. She was searching online for ideas when she came upon handmade cards with rolled paper strips. Intrigued, she made her first handmade card. Inspired, she decided to study this paper technique, otherwise known as Quilling or Paper Filigree.

Alyona is a Quilling Artist based out of Orange County, California, who originally started as a Business Analyst for fifteen years. With years of effort and passion put forth to master the Quilling craft, she is the founder, designer, and creator of Swirly Studio, as well as achieving artistic certification.

What started out as a hobby is now a thriving, creative business with a large following. Swirly Studio can be found on Instagram (@swirlystudio) where thousands follow for inspiration, tips, and tricks to learn more about Quilling.

Swirly Studio's original artwork is also available for purchase on their Etsy Shop. In her shop, Alyona creates personalized quilling art, greeting cards, earrings, miniatures, stemmed flowers, and more.

With the success of Swirly Studio across Social Media Platforms, Alyona decided to teach and inspire newcomers who desire to master the art of Quilling. Her teachings can be found on SkillShare, where she updates her curriculum with new classes every month. She loves teaching the most and expresses this as she watches her students perfect every swirl and coil, sees their excitement, gives them guidance as they practice, and encourages her students.

Alyona Kochubey believes Quilling is possible for everyone. All one needs to start is paper strips, glue, scissors, and background paper.

Production Team: Publishing Manager – Megan Copeland; Technical Editor – Lisa Lancaster; Graphic Artist – Katie Cooper-Bussell and Michael Puckett; Photo Stylist – Lori Wenger; Photographer – Jason Masters.

Made in U.S.A.